Your Face in the Fire

Poems

by

Naomi Ruth Lowinsky

BLUE LIGHT PRESS ◆ 1ST WORLD PUBLISHING

SAN FRANCISCO ◆ FAIRFIELD ◆ DELHI

Your Face in the Fire

Copyright ©2024 by Naomi Ruth Lowinsky

1st World Library
PO Box 2211
Fairfield, IA 52556
www.1stworldpublishing.com

Blue Light Press
www.bluelightpress.com
bluelightpress@aol.com

Book & Cover Design
Melanie Gendron
melaniegendron999@gmail.com

Cover Art
Kathleen Russ
kathleen@kathleenruss.com

Author Photo
Lorena Coelho

First Edition

Library of Congress Cataloging-in-Publication Data

ISBN: 978-1-4218-3560-0

Praise for Naomi Ruth Lowinsky's Poetry

(from *red clay is talking* – first book, 2000)

"Shifting, dappled light, interwoven with shadow. The colors of bright detail softened under moonglow. In Naomi Lowinsky's consistent search for the Mother, the meaning of the feminine, we meet the Goddess in her many guises. This is a poetry of quest, and the poet takes us through myriad ages and cultures. We partake with her in ecstasy and darkness, passion, epiphany and hunger, and our world is larger for it."

– Diane di Prima, author of *Revolutionary Letters* and *Loba*

"Naomi Ruth Lowinsky's *Your Face in the Fire* is a journey through the long and productive life of a well-recognized poet, a chariot traveling through timelessness. It is as much autobiographical as it is transcendent and timeless in its relationship to our collective unconscious. Here the reader encounters a goddess book, a mystical book, and a political book that speaks to the soul of all of us who have visited the realm of the dark feminine and the light of our joyous world. The poems speak to the reader and, in turn we speak to ourselves forming reminiscences of our ageless past. The words prompt us to remember the names of our ancestors and experience their living influence on us today: "Yours is the river of tongues we drink so we may remember." In Naomi's work we encounter Basho, Thom Gunn, Isis, Sophia and Ruby, the trickster, Don Sandner, her husband Dan, and so many other lustful and holy characters. Poems are Naomi's home where her spirit grows wild. She implores us, through example, to listen to all that calls, welcome the visits from the unrecognized, and dance with the spirits of the depths. In this volume, we recognize and are humbled by our desperate need for the poetic and are in ecstasy as we delve into the inner world of a guide to the oft inaccessible and inexpressible realms of our experience."

– Jeffrey Moulton Benevedes, Former Editor-in-Chief *Jung Journal: Culture & Psyche*

In Grateful Praise of *Your Face in the Fire.*

"Welcome to Naomi Ruth Lowinsky's world: a lamentation, a celebration, an eloquent unearthing of a lifetime's worth of memories and then some – achingly sacred, passionately profane, potently political: a reverential re-assembling, "from the bottom of life" on up, of the deepest, darkest, wildest and most ungovernable Feminine, rich root source of us all. I love how this poet of the depths, this dear soul sister, weaves together the sweetness and loneliness of childhood, the hot lure of bad boys and the tender triumph of aging soulmates, the tragic flame out of a town called Paradise, the greedy gutting of our precious Earth, "the Angel of Sciatica," odes to Hillary Clinton and whales and old cars. A bare-footed Elijah appearing, radiant, toasting the grandchildren who will inhabit this strange human future. The depth and grief and joy of Naomi's soul-retrieval lead us to wave our hands in the air—not unlike her third-grade classmates who called out, "Here!" to the morning rollcall—to show up for the unabashedly uncontrollable now, each moment indelibly etched in eternity once we rejoin the stars."

– Sharon Heath, author of *The Fleur Trilogy* and *The Mysterious Composition of Tears*

"Naomi Ruth Lowinsky's book of poetry: *Your Face in the Fire*, speaks with an impassioned voice which opens us up to that vast space which we find in Jung's Red Book. It is a vibrant standpoint from which she encounters the mysteries of the psyche. Through her poetic imagination we get to participate in her vision making process. Nourished by her dreams that invite us to imagine with her as she expresses a life time of creating, engaging, reflecting and reworking while showing us how her process is not only transformational for her, but for anyone who opens up to the reality of their experiences of psyche's being. The archetypal dimension shines through this book."

– Sam Kimbles, Ph.D., author of *Phantom Narratives* and *The Suffering of Ghosts*

"To read this book is to drink of a rare and holy elixir: an exuberant, deeply soulful life masterfully distilled into word music. If you read slowly and are lucky, you might fall into the alchemical vat with her, where your own life begins to crackle and shimmer in her light. In previous works, Naomi gorgeously, fearlessly answered the call of the ancestors to remember, to grieve, to embody, and to reclaim the pearls of grace left in the ruins of exile and shattered dreams. Here she sings her own long and inspired life, from starry vault to watery cave, from Zion to California to Mexico, with the same unflinching gaze and eye for beauty, where the goddess is found inside every stone, where even evil and death – including her own – are alchemized to serve as chiaroscuro revealing love's transfigurations over time. Her lamentations are so inseparable from her passionate, sensual exultations that they become the song of life itself, utterly intoxicated with the heartbreaking beauty of existence on Earth in the eyes of the soul. As a result, she writes, Elijah appears at the table: "*Here I am   says he/ Here you are.*""

– Frances Hatfield, PhD, LMFT, former poetry editor, *Jung Journal: Culture and Psyche;* author, *Rudiments of Flight.*

Also by Naomi Ruth Lowinsky

POETRY

Death and His Lorca
The Faust Woman Poems
Adagio and Lamentation
crimes of the dreamer
red clay is talking

POETRY CHAPBOOKS

The Little House on Stilts Remembers
Dreaming Night Terrors

PROSE

The Motherline: Every Woman's Journey to Find Her Female Roots
The Sister from Below: When the Muse Gets Her Way
The Rabbi, the Goddess, and Jung: Getting the Word from Within

ANTHOLOGIES

Soul Making in the Valley of the Shadow by the Deep River Poets
    (with Raluca Ioanid and Clare Cooper Marcus)
Marked by Fire: Stories of the Jungian Way
    (with Patricia Damery)

Agni is the mouth of the gods
The Vedas

*Support me for I stagger, drunk with fire…I climbed down
through the centuries and plunged into the sun at the bottom.
And I rose up drunk from the sun…*
C. G. Jung *The Red Book*

Table of Contents

Section Three: Why Am I Here?

For the many gone   who showed me my way

Fire is Your Name and Your Maker

Fire is your god's
eye gleam   the tiger that prowls your dreams
Fire is your sun   and your rising

You had to tamp your fire
down hard   back in the day of pointy bras
and girdles   when a spark in the back of a Chevy

could knock you up   Remember
when a fiery tongue could get you
burnt alive?

Fire in the hearth   now that's
a woman's business   embers
from Mother's fire   offerings

from the tree   kitchen fire
bedroom fire   birth fire   fire
from the core of the earth   When cauldron boils

there is no fire that can't escape   no fire
that will not leap and sass   change shape
be burning snake in summer grasses

hot breasted home wrecker
funeral pyre   I ask you
how do you keep from burning

your love to ashes?
I'll tell you how
Take a twig from the tree   Whittle a sharp tip

Mix Mother's fire with yours   Burn

Make ash marks
on white paper   Write yourself down

your leap and your sass   your hot breasted
double edged axe   the tiger that prowls your dreams
    your sun and your rising

Section One

The Gods We Were

Your Face in the Fire

Descend upon me   you who are source
before source   fire in the sky   gleam
in the back of my skull   Come in the wind
with wings   Come in my breath   I cling
to the luminous stair   Sing me your names
spirit   void   darkening sea   world
tree   When thunder speaks   come into my heart
where terrible stories are told
                                        The woman
whose womb has cast pieces of flesh   all over the streets
of Jerusalem   that son of your prophet   whose light
splintered   into thousands of dangerous
shards

          I gather it all for the altar
                              the blood   the rage   the weeping
                                        Show me your face
                                                    in the fire

Birth Day Poem 2017

Carry me back   through the laboring dark
into first light   first cry   first touch
of mother's hands   Those hands

broad palmed   big fingered   always working
kitchen hands   comfort hands   hands that tried
to stitch the world back together

when father erupted   the furies took over
It was the summer of '43   What did they know
my young parents   about the Europe they'd fled

the trains   the chimneys   What happened
to Father's mother   his father   his sister Maia   named
for that goddess who dances with veils   Some say

She's illusion   Some say She's creation
plays with imagination   Then rips
the magic carpet away

Carry me back to that cave   I clambered into
decades ago   hushed by the resonant dark
where ancient hands shaped   Her stony vagina   just so

at noon   on the Vernal Equinox   a ray of sun
would penetrate   Her innermost   Look
through the rocky lips   of Her vulva   the earth

bears fruit   Your little life   and mine   in the flow
of all the mothers of mothers   the grandmothers of magic
the daughters of ritual skill   who carry us   living and dead

Come   Sit with me by the fire   though bones ache
memory flickers   hands lose their hold
on the world   Those evil spirits   who spooked

my cradle   are back   The fire spits
and sputters   The furies   rave
and mutter   Here comes Maia

dancing in the flames   She who lit
the fire   of every life I've lived
has no patience   with lamentation   Shows me

her teeth   and I know   it is She
who will carry me out   through the laboring dark
when it's time   She

who will rip
the veils

Until then   I gather my harvest
love   laughter   dreams   poems
This one's for Her

Memory Old Trickster

What have you done with the names
of my playmates   the twins
who galloped   whinnied   tossed radiant manes
in the wild horse woods   when we were eight?

What have you done with the faces
my third-grade teacher's   and every child
who sat in rows   saying "here"
when she called out our names?

Where have you hidden the secret life
of the girl who used to be me   the one who'd spend hours
in the world of some book   'til mother yelled   "You've been
                                                                cooped up

all day   Get out in the sun and play!"

I've lost the flow of her daydreams   You've cut me off
from her longing   Don't get me wrong
I'm grateful   for every flash of the past
you reveal with a sweep of your cape

You've given me back the oak
roots for wandering words
song of wind and leaves
soothe my sun dazzled eyes

You've given me back the willow   green hair
of lament and longing   sweet spot
where a girl learned to ride
the one she was meant to become

You've cast the spell of my first bad boy lover   the one
who released me from nice girl jail   to a world of weed

and wild men   then lost me in Old Man Skinner's garage
to one who could fix my sad sack Saab

That was most of a lifetime ago   now you lose me and find me
and lose me again   in this shell game you call my life
O remember me back to that sweet spot   goddess mound
                                        tree of my life
                                        wild horse
                                        I'll ride
                                                'til I'm done

The State of California

1. Shape Shift

I can see me now   a scrawny girl   in a brick row house
in Queens

where no woman rules   where no tree beckons
where only the catfish   in the murky pond   quickens
my breath   It is here   my body turns stranger
to me   Breasts blossom   Mother spots blood
in my underwear   Moon   puts her moody spell on me
with achy   belly   fingers   Father's fiat
"We're moving to California"   shifts me into
pre-teen emergency   I might as well be   the lone survivor
of a firestorm   friends gone   my Rapid Progress
ladder   to high   intelligentsia skies
burned down   to blackened ground   And yet

the word   California
is music   on my tongue
gives me visions
of a land   where dark-skinned women
with weapons of gold   ride wild horses
under luminous skies   There are palms
and fruit trees   just walk out and pick your own
apples   pomegranates   apricots
The Rose Garden lures me   off the path
to school   among the redwoods' intoxicating
pine smell   I hear my own   self   sing
The Golden Gate gleams   The bay glitters

2. Seeing Lessons

There are no ebony Amazons   in the land   of California
where Oma lives   in a house with an arched   window
she paints the glow   of golden light   in the room

where she's hung   her portrait of Opa   reading Dickens
He dropped dead   playing chess   soon after they'd arrived
refugees   in this sanctuary state   Generations later
cousins of cousins will tell me   he saved their families
wrote warnings   sent money   robbed the death camps

I see Oma still   her raven eyes   her north wind breath
her passion   raises her brush   into the trees
the breeze   swiftly shapes a single   California poppy
its many fingered leaves   grasp the sun
its vase   is a smudge of gray   She tracks
the changing light   of her reflection   from melancholia   to self
possession   tracks my mood   knows when
the dark of the moon
has got me   On Saturdays she shows me
and my best friend Cathy   how to sketch   how to see
It's all about shadow   Shadow shapes
the teacup   the pomegranate   the kitchen towel
Shadow shapes   the world

Oma worries   about the weather
No rain   in November   Must be
that atom bomb testing   in the desert

3. What Kind of Promised Land?

When I finally dare to look   into his eyes   I see the light
as though we have descended   from the dust
of the same star   Some angel   has the grace to whisper
Get off your high horse   Tell him you feel vulnerable
On account of all the love   I've lost   the ties   I've squandered
                                                    the lust
that flamed and burned   for bad boy charmers   one note
                                                    flutists
the ring a ding of metal   striking metal   when flesh denies
its wounds   I never seem to learn   until I dare to look

and see his soul   is looking back
We two have been home to one another   ever since
that summer day   a kind of Eden
I never dared imagine   though by November

we've descended   into an underworld   The People's Temple
is no utopia   It's a death camp   A white man   whose words
are golden   has led his   mostly   dark-skinned followers
who have no weapons   who have no gold
into the jungle he calls Paradise   singing
Death be your angel   Death be your sweet   swing low chariot
Death be your Mother and Child Reunion   carrying you home
Then come the assassinations shocked ghosts of Mayor
                                                                    Moscone
Supervisor Milk   broken spirits   of power to the people
gunned down   in the city of Saint Francis
by some Twinkie crazed   former cop   named White
What kind of promised land is this?

And yet   by summer   we two stand   under the umbrella elm
in the presence of the tall palm   in the garden   behind the big
                                                                    house
the rabbi blesses our delight   We promise each other   the
                                                                    moon
the deep roots of the Tree of Life   in the presence of
my parents   his parents   my children   his children
still haunted by the marriages   we left

4. Altar

Lifetimes later   the children   mostly gone
though someone always has   an emergency
We pick up the big old house   shake it out
take off through the tunnel   to the other side
A high ridge   golden hills   luminous skies   and
if we crane our necks   Devil Mountain

The great horned owl   hoots in the night   across the valley
her mate hoots back   We watch the sun's passage
north in summer   south in winter
We pour red wine unto the earth   say *Pachamama*
Deer dare   to climb our front steps   devour
our geraniums   as my shadow flickers
in the glass door   they leap away   into coyote brush

Those are the years   when great cats stalk
my dreams   slash my writing hand   demand poetry
the years when night sweats   heat lightening
thunder   me awake   and the dark skinned one
blessed be She   emerges from her cave   speaks
from the world   before the word   was written

This wooden house   is an altar
makes sacred   the pilgrimage of the sun
the screech   of the hawk   the chant
of the frogs at dusk   but I tell you
this is no sanctuary
this is the kind of house
the fire will take

5. Dark Roots

Were there a tense   in English
as there is in Quechua   for altered states
for dreamtime   would you follow me

through the veil?

She comes to me   in the dark   this beauty
from the bottom of time
before Abraham and Sarah   left Ur
before Africa wept   for her stolen children
before wrong way Columbus   stumbled into
an unexpected realm   of Arawak people   with copper skin
with fertile gods

13

She rode the ocean currents   all the way
from Africa   to the land we now call   America
with her army of Amazons   their gold tipped spears
wrathful   wise   weird   teller of terrible truths
She violates   space   time   transgresses
the borders   of myth   dream   reverie

What is She doing   in the dreams of an aging
Ashkenazi Jew   as the black goddess   Isis
as Sophia   with Ethiopian features
as Ruby   who takes me in   to her warm home
in a bad part of town   Jim Crow keeps messing with her
but she can talk story   all the dreaming night long

We all emerge from the dark
We all emerge   from one Mother
Long ago   there was a Queen   named Califia
She gave her sacred name   to the State
of California   Listen to Her   She is our ancestor

6. Queen Califia Gets Her Say

Dreams   are the fruit   of your tree   the roots
of your dark   If you walk with me   through the veil
I'll show you the cave   of the lingam   or perhaps it's
the phallic headed goddess   anointed in wise blood
I'll call forth the spirits   of the daughters   of my daughters
who lived in this valley   where you now   make your nest
They wove baskets   so strong   they could hold water
so strong   they could hold   fire heated stones
cook acorn mush   They knew the waning
and the waxing moon   the solitude   their daughters needed
to hold the mysteries   while the moon ebbed away
and the old women covered   the young ones' heads
with deer skin   to keep the chaos in   For the dark of the moon
was taboo   that achy descent   into womb   was taboo

14

meaning   it was sacred   to close their eyes
to sit on high   to keep their feet   above the earth
to keep the wild ride   deep inside   to conjure me
the dark queen   from whom they are descended
keeper of the golden   yoni flower
maker of worlds   reader of earth mind
river mind   ocean mind   forest mind

with its dreams of fire

Long gone now   my daughters
and so I come to you   in my uncanny mode   in my fury
about greed   about power grabs   about predatory mind
which devours   forests   mountains   species
You want power? I'll show you power   Just watch me
a being of pure electricity   a pillar of brimstone   ablaze with fire
from my crazed hair   to the blackened earth

beneath my feet

7. Paradise

If you're lucky   old love becomes   a kind of Eden
though his bones ache   on waking
though my toes forget   how to grab
the floor   as I stumble to turn off   Chopin's nocturne
which has been rousing us   for decades   though the angel
with the scythe   shows up from time-to-time   leering
at our easy delight   our wordplay banter   our deep rooted
wide branched   tree of knowing   which shelters us   for the

times
are nasty   soldiers sew up   the southern border   with

concertina wire
by order of the President   children are ripped away
from their families   seeking sanctuary   in fear   in trembling

I walk around our quiet meander   rolling green paths
through redwoods   palms   townhouses

15

to the laurel   from which I can usually see   the mountain
is swallowed up   by sulfuric smoke   the habitations of Paradise
its treasure   its creatures   its trees   incinerated   this terrible
                                                    November
the air is filled with ash   our mouths are gritty   our lungs ache
everything is veiled   in heavy mourning   the hills   the vine-
                                                    yards
the twisted winding road   we're driving   to see Sam and Sara
who almost lost their lives   in last years'   wine country fires
the State of California   is an emergency
the sun is a blood   red   ball   casts a pall
                                on everything that breathes

If breath is how the Holy One   gives body   to our souls
how do we sit still   keep the chaos inside
how do we conjure   Queen Califia   Her ebony horse women
those who remember   only the magic of fire   can release
                                the seeds of tomorrow?

To a Kinsman from Before the Divide

Irony gleams   in your eyes   Africa glows
in your skin   You're not smiling   in the yearbook photo
Neither am I   We were kin   in the tribal lands
of High School   Belonged to the intelligentsia   Argued
existentialism   civil disobedience   Mutually Assured

Destruction   Yours the wise   crack   wit   Yours
the panther   mind   How you loved   knocking down
my idols   I must have looked   like Pollyanna
standing before   the assembly   pleading my earnest plan
to desegregate the student government   You knew

that few   on either side   of the divide
would give a damn   We never spoke
of Emmet Till   too close   to your terror
We never spoke   of my crazy Aunt Ljuba
from Bergen Belsen   We never spoke

of sex   You kept your secret   in the closet   Nor did I tell you
my father was concerned   about us   always together
I tried to tell him   it wasn't like that   Then what
was it like?   Why do I miss you to this day?
The truth is   with you   I was free to be

strong minded   loud mouthed   a bitch
on wheels   Just the kind   my father despised
After graduation   I lost you
lost me   found me anew
when the goddess swept through   and poetry began

Once I heard you   on the radio
a distinguished professor of history   To my delight
you proclaimed America   a "mongrel nation"

17

I called you up   You weren't interested   in what's
become of me   I guess you've had your fill

of bleeding-heart Jews   But now
after Orlando   after Charlottesville
after Sandra Bland   Michael Brown   Trayvon Martin   after
Jews   Will Not   Replace Us
I need your irony   your terrible knowing
                              your idol   smashing   wit

Because of What Aches

Because your neck tries to rise above
a tangle of Gordian knots

Because your cranky knuckles know why
your grandmother fumbled with buttons   with jar lids

Because your knee   like the knee of your father before you
can prophesy rain

Because it's late May
but it's acting like a nasty winter day

Because your hips are as surly
as a girl at fourteen   fire tamped down and smoking

Though you've given yourself to the wild ride
Chased toddlers drunk wine   had words with the owl on the roof

Because you're as beaten by weather   as the gnarled willow
which creaked in the night   then split

Because there are so many sagas   not yet lived
you're not ready   for ash or thin air

Because your eyes long   for the mountain
and the old rose   still blooms

Ask the fire to take your early drafts
your irritable reaching after   what's not yours

because of what aches

To the Lady and Her Poet

All pleasures and all pains, remembering
The bough of summer and the winter branch.
     "Sunday Morning" – Wallace Stephens

1.
Oracular   the filtered light of oak
through her peignoir   She comes to me as though
her spell was never broken   I'm still twenty
I can smell   those pungent oranges in the sun
Did I get lost?   Did I forget?   Her music
is a river long gone underground   The lady dreams me
as a girl   seated in an oak   enraptured
by the "chaos of the sun"

2.
Did I forget?   Did I get lost   in "the dark
encroachment of that old catastrophe?"
The river flows from forest into cave
Listen   "the ancient hush of holy sacrifice"
There was a shattering   The old gods severed
by stroke of axe   The shadows brood
about the gone   the lost   The waters
wander on   into the "chaos of the sun"

3.
Sun and drops of rain after a long drought
The lady speaks for birds   and for the alphabet
of trees   *Remember   one mid-summer   a door*
opened?   You found your self with me
beneath the hazel tree?   Nine branches
each one a muse   We gathered seeds
to feed the salmon   Your thoughts were wings
amidst "the chaos of the sun"

4.
Seated in the same old chair   that held me
when first I met   my lady's gaze
Did I get lost?   Did I forget?   Her musings
are my own "green wings"   What use the smell
of oranges   the memory of oak invoked peignoir
when years wheel to the thirteenth tree   the elder
the tree of death?   How does a poet of the old enchantment
sing us through   this shattering
                              into the "chaos of the sun"?

To My Long Ago Lady Delight

Before you and the Serpent stopped being holy
Before Adam laid claim to cattle and hawk

Before you preferred exile with demons
to lying beneath him

Before Eve sank her teeth into God's own fruit
Before lust abandoned me

There was a time   my Lilith

when you were my own honey cave
My snake in the fervent grass

O Lady of mango breasts
of hips that reach for the moon

How long has it been since you sang
in my blood?

Come back to me on screech owl wings   Soar free
of your Red Sea spell

the time you've done
in wet dreams

I long for you   in my wildflower bed
Bring me your fire

Full Circle with Goddess

for Judy Grahn

When I take your goddess incantation   off the shelf
where She's lived   in relative obscurity   for over forty years
wandering the wilds   at the back of my mind   while I sit
among decades of notebooks   *The Collected   The Selected*
myriad voices   who sing me   into my self
I suddenly hear   Her holler   *She WHO*
She   she She   she She   she WHO?

How could I forget   what a wallop She packs
howls   hoots   questions   answers
a Goddess of breath   of high desert wind
wind off the lake   wind on the mountain
blows off   the top of my head   I'm hanging on
to the tail of a tiger   whipping me back
to that twenty something   I was
when I stood on a stage with you   Judy
howling   hooting   asking   answering
It was Berkeley   1972
We'd all suddenly remembered   the one we forgot
who cradled us   though we denied Her
for we had not yet grasped   that small clay goddess
from Willendorf   who fits   in a woman's hand
You conjured Her   Judy
She Who turns things over

The earth opened   It was our period
We raised our fists   We wanted the moon
and the moon wanted us
Everything changed   Nothing changed
What happened   to that radiant glimpse
did She slip   out of our grasp   like a waning moon

while Big Oil drilled down deep
because power is power
because nothing is sacred
when all that counts is speed   is greed
yet each of us still goddess bound
made the descent down below down into menstrual mind
Me tracking our mothers' mothers' mothers
into the forbidden where *She Who* reigns
You riding the moonboat into long ago
where a girl sits in the dark of her first blood
bearing the chaos creating the world   Ah Judy
though we never met again have we not come full circle

are we not olden olden olden
are we not belly full of wise blood
are we not heart sick with dread
watching the chaos take over our world

She Who floods like a river
packs a wallop when she's wounded
She thunders roars runs rivers through the skies
runs hot runs cold runs dry Breathes fire
Where is home?

She Who is the first person to no other
takes me back to our fore mother
the one in the cave painting
the galloping poetry mare you still ride
I still ride her mane flying
in the wind off the lake
                    we're both hanging on

The Gods We Were

Once you were a god   I remember
such delight
in your eyes   in your laugh

in your hands that knew how
to release me
into the wild

in every world we travelled
tropical island   redwood grove
river flow over the falls

I was your goddess
with radiant breasts
You were my stallion
with wings   remember?

Now that you're human   and so am I
with backs that ache
and weary feet   we meet

after separate days   at twilight
You've roasted a chicken
with tarragon and thyme

I slice a persimmon
you picked from our tree
to toss in a salad

We decide which wine

These days the gods
are our children's children

We worship them
but what is most holy is this
slow domestic dance
this wistfulness of ending days

What remains in the gathering dark
this gift from the gods
we used to be   such delight
                              remember?

Serenissima's Embrace

The beauty is not the madness
                    – Ezra Pound

It's the pigeons   their fervent fluttering
their lovesick crooning   who charm you into this
                                    Venetian trance

A black boat glides   through gray green water
Every stone bridge   has its lovely
her naked shoulders   her boy friend in straw hat
She holds her selfie stick just so   Gazes at herself   and him
                                    with Facebook eyes

Our Lady of Serenity leads you on   turns you round
loses you   confuses you   shifts scenery when you're not looking
Alleys devour you   feed you to other alleys
Map can't find you   Smart phone tracks you
                                    to the middle of the lagoon

Our Lady was stolen from Byzantium

Our Lady used to be a great queen   Bought and sold nations
Now she has nothing better to do   than to twiddle
your compass   agitate your tides   spit you out   into the
                                    blinding babble
of the hordes   reeling with spinners   while sun does its
                                    glitter thing
on the Grand Canal   and the shrouded   the scaffolded Basilica
          raises its many heads   on the Piazza San Marco

His body was stolen from Alexandria

We are here We have always been here We will always be here
Oblivious to what the old man on the stone bench foresees

As it was   so it will be
Falling towers   Rising seas

If only you could rise above the tangle
of footpaths and waterways   on the wings of that lion
If only you could soar through the millennia   with big cat feet
well versed in air currents   tides   the lost book of magic
high above towers   cupolas   swing low around the backside
of wonder   swoop down down   into the dream of the lagoon
you'd hear Byzantium singing   in hushed gold

Through a high arch   Noah maneuvers his ark

Spirit stirs the waters   The lost   the homeless
the ones who have seen it all   towers falling   seas rising
The ones who learned to fish   in marshlands
The ones who figured out how   to pierce the sea floor
with a bristling forest of logs   that hold up the glowing
water veined body   of Our Lady

A city was stolen from the sea

Our Lady gathers you   murmurs in your ear   "No one knows
what fate is hidden in the lion's mouth   or when your time
                                        will come
                              to do the bone dance"

It's the pigeons   their fervent flutterings
their lovesick crooning   who charm you into this
                              Venetian
                                 Siren Song

At the Red Sea

To those who remember when we were slaves
how we were broken   in Pharoah's grip
To those who stand   at the Red Sea's edge
and cannot imagine the other side   who've forgotten
the voice in the burning bush   forgotten
the angel before we were born   can't imagine
the song of Miriam

To those who hid   under our desks
covered the back of our necks
imagined the unimaginable   blasting
our world into radiant dust

To those who could never believe
we'd have children   our children would have children
For we had seen the hole in the sky
rivers burn   bee colonies collapse
To those who are sick   of imagining
yet another unimaginable
end of the world   I say

Breathe   Notice   we have survived
There are doves in the garden
The apple tree blooms
Our grandchildren sit round the Seder table
We've opened the door   for Elijah
Poured him a good glass   of Zinfandel

We never expected to see *him* walk in
His feet are bare
His face is a marvel of radiant dust
He spreads his wings above us   raises his glass

to the granddaughters
to the grandsons

Here I am   says he
Here you are

You Without Name Without Face

I wait for you at sunset
I have heard of your green flash

I look for your delicate hands in the dark
making the music of stars

I wait for you in temples
The rabbis say you are One

But you keep changing your shape
pillar of cloud   chariot   tree

I hear you at the chalice well
you murmur to me in water

You tug at my feet at Avebury
The old stones remember you

You show me illuminated manuscripts
maps of the ends of the earth

I look for you in dreams
You write with fire

> *Where are you after the blinding flash*
> *after the shattering?*

Flood I know   and wildfire
wind that uproots trees

but you
of the burning bush

you
of the mountain top

you
beyond sight   and sense

How can I know   You?

Demeter Beside Her Self

I've been thrown out of orbit
spilled out of holy grail
My used to be darling daughter's   gone off
                            like a powder keg

If Hades had grabbed her you'd see me
sitting on a rock   refusing flowers
refusing the fruit of the vine
                     until she's returned to me

If Krishna had swept her away
in the fragrant night   I'd remember
the Gopi girl I used to be
                     and wish her joy

But she's off becoming
someone I've never been   after yelling at me
that my endless rounds   lovers babies grandbabies
                   are totally suffocating

She wants power   she wants digital devices
She wants electricity all night long
Is there an underworld
               in virtual space?

What's the sun to do   or the moon
if round and round is out
of fashion?   And me?   There is no rock can hold
                       my fury

My used to be darling daughter
is riding a rocket to Mars   You'll know me
as fire on the mountain   You'll know me
                   storming your beaches

for I've been thrown out of orbit
spilled out of holy grail
My used to be darling daughter's   gone off
                                    like a powder keg

Joker's Wild

When I've retreated to my sanctuary
lit the candle   followed my breath

from noisy garbage can collection
to the Hidden Door   Why is it You

Old Wise Guy of Creation   who shows up
where light leaps   where music soars   Why You

the Bad Boy in the temple   Why You
who won't take off your shoes

who track coyote shit
into the Holy of Holies?   You

who upset my donkey cart   throw pits
upon the sacred mound

who mix the holy
and the smelly everyday   You

bag of windy farts   You
who make the dandelions laugh

so hard they scatter seed   Why You
my dangerous   my Holy Fool   who

fill me with ridiculous exuberance   You
amulet against the Evil Eye   You

with the blindfold and the violin   You
lure me to the edges of the known

show me the Abysmal Jaws
of Crocodile   and say

Leap

Thanks

Blessed art Thou, no One
      – Paul Celan

for what you do with light O concealed of the concealed
behind closed eyelids white shimmers
yellow swirls a green vine crosses the abyss Thanks
for the loan of breath your company down the tree
      your every hallelujah leaf twenty two paths
        many singing names down down
          past the purple belly of the moon
            to the concrete city where
            we have lamented
                Sophia and I

  Machinery snarls Money hisses No One's child
  is in the temple No One sings thanks to you
  No One's root finds the wet in the dark no One's
     word speaks
        a tree lives in no One's eye

Angelology

The Angel of Now is named
Sciatica   She's got you

under her irritated sway
The Angel of Hurry has mislaid

your glasses   She's a black hole
full of lost keys   lost worlds

last night's forgotten dream

The Angel whose name is Presence
can't find your voice   gets stuck

in your blind alleys   Your hip complains
of cranky weather   Your shoulders ache
                                        to be wings

The Angel of The Times breaks into
your glass house   shatters

your favorite bubble   smears fear
all over the news

This Angel is a Banshee
with a Hammer

This Angel is the Radiant Eye
                              Look

The persimmon tree hangs heavy with fruit
Rain glistens on leaves   turning red   turning gold

Breath deep   from your belly
Smell the wet earth

So speaks the Angel
from Before You Were Born

Remember me?   I'm the one
who promised you
                              all this

Only the Blind

You have always belonged to the moon
Though sometimes it leads you astray

Past willows across the swinging bridge
To somebody's grave by the river

Stuck in the cave of your skull
You grope for the disappeared moon

Down where it's blue so blue
Only Blind Willie Johnson

Can sing your way home
Only Isaac the Blind can see

The banshee has got your bones
She's beating her drum with your bones

And you're stuck in the cave of your skull
No willows no swinging bridge

Who will plant you deep in the earth?
Who will water your toes?

When the banshee has got your bones
When she's beating her drum with your bones

You have always belonged to the moon

Only Isaac the Blind can show you
That glow beyond the bridge

Only Blind Willie Johnson
Can sing your way home

Section Two

Lust and the Holy

Why Rabi'a Won't Sleep

In the dark   when everyone's asleep   when nobody commands
Fetch this   Carry that   Feed the camels   Water the ass

Pour holy water out of all the vessels   Beat the magic
out of all the carpets   Wash the Sultan's dirty underwear

In the dark   the only time I have to be
with the stars   with my breath

with the moonlit beat
of my feet   the reed flute wail

of my longing for You   Sing to me
and I will wrap my slave girl arms

around the amazement   of You
                              and dance

                    in the dark

What She Says to Her Old Mother India

Are you still there?   Long ago
you took a grindstone   to my certainties
Red and purple no longer clash
The many are One

Are you still there?
Long ago you wrapped me in saris
heated me up 'til I was fragrant
as cinnamon and chilies

then cut off my head
one of the many
rattling skulls
for your necklace

My arms grew long to wrap around you   mother

Are you still there?
Long ago you revealed to me
your black idol
under the banyan tree

women's toilet
women's shrine
She was garlanded with marigolds
offered cigarettes and ghee

You sang me a song that never ended   mother
until I left you for the West   long ago

They say there is a highway now
that wraps you round
with Tata Nanos   fuming trucks
where once were bullock carts

bicycle rickshaws   a skinny cow
taking a nap in the middle
of the road
They say there are glass towers

24/7 work weeks
software wallahs on the telephone
to America
where once Ganesha danced

If this is so
when does Vishnu sleep
who churns the ocean of milk
who sings Krishna

of the jingling anklets   all night long?
My arms grew long to wrap around you   Mother
long ago
Are you still there?

In the School of Desire

Theft was your teacher   The chocolate you stole
from Mother's secret place   taught you to taste
dark   milk   bittersweet

The books you devoured in stolen time
not doing your job   in the library stacks
gave you the low down   on love

in every position   You stole yourself far
from Father's compass   Lost North   waylaid West
travelled East   South took you on a ride   a stowaway

on other people's myths   You lusted
after dark gods   lost wax gods
carved in ebony gods   gods with myriad arms

That was lifetimes ago
Now you're old   still studying
in the school of desire   You thank every god

you stole   every god who transported you
out of cubicles   traffic jams   bad breath encounters
with insular minds   You make offerings

of bittersweet chocolate and wine   love
in any position still possible
though you know

that Dark God   that thief beyond
the bedroom window   bides
                             his sweet time

Me Too

September 27th 2018

All of us are you   Christine   in this moment
All of us in tears   because that's what we do   when we're mad
All of us took off the day   to watch you tell
what few of us have ever dared   to tell
All of our eyes dart   from senator   to prosecutor
Prosecutor?   Whose nightmare is this?

Some of us watched Anita Hill   face those same   white men
those same   dead fisheyes   a generation ago   Anita was so
self possessed   Not one hair   went astray   in her careful do
while your scared hair   Christine   blows around   tangles
in your eye glass frames   tries to hide
the terrified fifteen-year-old   in you we all are
For who of us has not felt   that heavy hand   over our mouth
Who of us has not feared   death by suffocation?
Who of us has not heard   that nasty laughter?

Shirley Chisholm locked herself   in chambers   Wept her rage
at those old boys   who dismissed   diminished   betrayed her
They could not tolerate   a Black woman   running for president
Who of us did not feel   primordial fear   when Hillary spoke up
while the guy with that schlong of a tie   stalked her   mocked her
Who of us did not feel   the hot tongs   of the Inquisitor
when in the Quicken Loans Arena   in Cleveland   in 2016
a guy with a tie incited the crowd to "Lock Her Up!" "Lock Her Up!"

All of us know what happens   to those who refuse to do
the patriarchal dance   of diffidence
We're stalked   pilloried   diagnosed as disturbed
in the womb   We bleed from our eyes
Well you're showing them   Christine   not one iota

47

of rage   not a drop   of disturbance   You make sweet and pliant
eye contact   name your terror   though sometimes we glimpse
the owl in your soul   how your roots reach down   to your own
                                                          hard truth

You're a flower in a fierce wind   pulling petals in close   until
storm over   goddess willing   you rise
to your full stature   dismiss the security detail   return
to your everyday home with its two front doors teach psychology
make dinner   walk the dog   help the boys with their homework

But this is not the end of it   Your dance of diffidence
settles nothing   He's back   the one we all remember from forever
beating his chest   roaring   No one stops
his predatory attack   his entitled engorgement   for which we are
a handy piece of flesh   to be grabbed   groped   banged   nailed

                                        to a broken
                                                  branch
                                                        of the tree

All of us know   what he's not saying
that we're witches   bitches   we are   let's say it aloud
CUNTS   And what is a cunt   but a portal   into a new world
we all come through   unless Caesar gets his way
and what is a witch   but a woman of power
who knows her own nature   is a part of all nature

In my dream a brilliant Black girl paints the world in every living color
She's Changing Woman   Woman of the Craft   Woman becoming us all
She runs strong as a wild horse   dodges rocks and fissures   Maybe
it's your dream Christine and we're all with you on the wings of the owl
in the deepest part of the woods   where the oak grove remembers
the ones we were before
                        we were grabbed   groped   banged   nailed

48

Banshee Under Your Skin

for Betty

You who descend   from women
who sat   vulva to earth   and bled
into the fields   Women who knew
our seat on this ground   is holy
Women who walked   barefoot
into the chasm   where snake is god
where even the animal shriek
                of sacrifice   is holy

Women who met ourselves
clambering out   of earth's mouth
where flesh rots   where stink rises
bearing   our ritual carnage
Women who knew   this too
even our agony song   even our fury
                       is holy

Listen to me
I have known you   forever
Unveil   those snake eyes
Unleash   that flickering tongue   Slough off
that dried old skin   Reveal
the shrieking banshee   you've been holding in
                       for thousands of years

Who stole our seat   in the world
broke our mothers   groped our daughters
covered our heads   so the moon   could not touch us
                filled our bodies   with shame?

Remember yourself   a woman descended   from women
who danced   to the rhythms of moon

knew the cave   where the wild fig grows
Yours the seductive   enchantment of snake
Yours the radiant   pulse of the drum
Yours   the mud–born lotus   and the holy woman
                              just under your skin   She's you

Lust and the Holy

I lust for you at sunset
Your gold   your shimmer
I crave your wild display
Your crimson   your fuchsia   your peach
I yearn for you on the mountain
I want what you give to the moon
I want to know you carnally
in every form of the holy
Elephant-headed Ganesha
wrap your trunk around me
Blue-stained Krishna
meet me where the lotus blooms
Mantis   Coyote   Raven
show me the tricks of desire
And you   O nameless one   you fire
that is never consumed
make me your temple dancer
woo me with sacred wine
I'll follow you even into the church
of the agonized god
in hushed light
with guttering candles
at evensong
I'll pray for you
O my dusky enchantment
be wilderness for me   be rainforest
be long line of pelicans dipping
wing tips into the surf
do not abandon me to concrete
to traffic lights
to skies abuzz with planes
where no gold shimmers
where city lights have bleached out
all your color
and I am lost
to lust and the holy

L.A. Reverie

City of lascivious skies
Can't keep your hands to yourself
Getting it on with the bougainvillea
Arousing the hanky pank palms

Can't keep your hands to yourself
Where ocean gets naked with sky
Our hanky pank palms do a chorus line kick
Singing the body fantastic

Where ocean gets naked with sky
Over and under the 405
Singing the body fantastic
A skateboarder leaps and twirls

Over and under the 405
Through canyons up mountains
Our skateboarder crouches careens
While sirens wail

Through canyons up mountains
Over red crested roofs and Spanish arches
While sirens wail
A purple baboon holds forth

Over flat roofs and Spanish billboards
In the city of flaunting your stuff
Our purple baboon holds forth
Telling stories of pity and terror

In the city of flaunting our stuff
We look for ourselves at the movies
Telling stories of pity and terror
Breasts swell   muscles ripple

We look for ourselves at the movies
Getting it on with the hanky pank palms
Breasts swell   muscles ripple
Under lascivious skies

To My Brother's Late Dragon Lady

So many sagas   come
and gone   since you and I strode
the '70s

Sister–out–law

High boots   high skirts
You with your Nikons
Me with my notebook

Free lancers

to the counterculture
High on sass and chutzpah
We got the low down

on the Cult of 'Do Jelly'

Me   just free
of marriage   You
never believed in it

Did the wild thing

with whomever
Lived with my brother
in perpetual

high drama

Plates flew
Cats cowered
Yours was the tongue of fire

He paid you back   big time

So many sagas come
and gone   That woman
he left you for

threw a few plates of her own   He left her

for some Delilah   younger
than my daughters
She took him on a ride

And my brother?

You escaped his saga
before you had to see him
alone and rotting

in a flea bag motel
in Venice
Back in the day   he knew everyone

Scored a case of Chateau Neuf de Pape

from the year you were born
Wheeler dealer   glad hand host
at your thirtieth birthday party

Listen Nikki   you're what eats him

Who knew   you'd have no life without him
Dragon would devour you
Forty never find you

In his nursing home

He tells me the same old same old story
I was the one who gave her
her first Nikon

I was the one who made her
a great photographer

But I'm the one you backlit
in black and white   showing the world
how to wrap a sari

                                      bare breasted

A River Flows Through Zion

for Dan

Thanks to you   our morning kitchen glows
   last night's dishes   have all   gone back   to their cupboards
    In the evening   it's a party   We toast each other   our
                            children
     our grandchildren   our complicated kith and kin   living
                           and dead
     Often there's music   The ghost of your father   loves
                          Tchaikovsky
     The ghost of my father   protests *That's kitsch   Give me*
                          Bach
     Give me Palestrina   After dinner   your mother's ghost
    shows up   admonishing   *Stay awhile   the dishes can*
                          wait
   This is so lovely   Does she know   she's quoting Goethe?
   My mother   recently departed   counsels
 You need to know   how lucky you are   Thanks to you   Dan
 I do   You're always there   when the printer jams   when the
computer torments me   Patient with machines   patient with me
you are sanctuary   you are roots in the earth   practical   solid
 and yet you are Coyote   You always see   the funny side
  You practice magic   conjure travel   Thanks to you
   we find ourselves   among towering   red cliffs
    deep canyons   creations of the Virgin River
     enacting the drama   of eternity   in constant flux
    You plotted this trip   You drove through the rain and
                       the hail
   This is Zion   the Promised Land   in the red state of Utah
  in the middle of   shaken with sorrow   and terror   America
  we sink   into our elements   Old Navajo Sandstone   river
                         flow
   rock of ages   light   of ancient stars   The river sings our stories
from the early days   of urgent embrace   to these gray-haired days

of reminiscence   even as reality   unravels   and the black hole
    prophesies

       End of the world   up ahead

You prefer   not to go there   You say   listen to the river
  you say   "Where shall we go for dinner?"   Lucky me
    I found a love who   as the river shapes stone
      has shaped my life   into a happiness   I never foresaw
        a love who speaks   geology   anthropology   musicology
                    who's even joined me   in speaking Jungian
        A love   who loves   the long flow   of language
      who'll follow words deep   into their undergrounds
                     where poetry begins
      where the tree of life grows   its roots   in the sky   it's branches
    touch earth   where we two play   with words
  as others bounce   a basketball   We know we've scored
        when Old English   and Old Norse   collaborate to tell us
Happiness   comes from "hap"   meaning chance   meaning luck
  In German   my first tongue   *Glück* is *"luck"* **and** *"happiness"*
  in one round word   which takes me back   to our old argument
Who's the lucky one?   You liked to tell me   it was you
    I'm here to tell you   *I'm the lucky one*   Long ago   you said
    you had a lot of love   to give   I wondered   *Really?*
    Unaccustomed as I was   to men   who claimed love
    as their forte   I'm here to say   your word is good
  "Good"   from Old English   Old German   to unite   join   fit
    Thanks to your   quick wit   your radiant charm   I've learned to play
"Play"   from roots that mean   engage   and pledge
as we did eons ago   *for better or worse   in sickness and in health*
There was a time   you felt   abandoned   Poetry had stolen me away
  We fought over time together   time apart   It took us time
    to reconcile   our differences   *"difference" from the root "bher"*
    as in to bear a child   as in to endure   also mouth   of the river
    fertile ground   where   thanks to you   poems flow

and you   send them out   into the world   Who knew?
          a bond can be a path   to freedom   Who knew?
          that *"thanks" and "think"   stem from the same root*
     Counter intuitive   right?   You'd think   thanks   belongs to
                                                                heart
          and think   to the busy mind   Thanks to your   cool head
                                                           warm heart
     I get it   You're a throw back   to a time   when head and heart
     were not yet   severed   Perhaps you are   a throw forward
to a future   where a man can love   as well as plan   as well as
                                              unjam printers
     Who knew?   when we stood   under the umbrella elm
          behind the big   old Oakland house   how far   how deep
          our roots would reach   way down to the Paleolithic
          high up   in the Rhodope Mountains   where Orpheus sings
          deep into Zion   where a waterfall   graces the red cliffs
          of the Temple of Sinawava   *Paiute word for Coyote*
     Thanks to you   Dan   I've learned the roots   of love
     desire and care   as one would expect   but who knew?
     love is related   to words that mean   give leave   permission   believe
                                                            trust
Thanks to you   the river flows through   our Rock of Ages
                                   our great   good   luck

59

Late in Love

The body gets cranky   hips lament   knees argue   hands
become ancient maps   Making love requires a strategy
of pillows   Touch me where I ache   Tomorrow
is a sly intruder   Remember me to the hours

that cup our wine   It's been years since the blood
thundered   Whose shadow will be first to fall?   The cards say
our work is done   The shovel is at rest   The cards say
there's more to come   Look how this day brims over

The fountain you tend is a psalm   It sings
to the stones and the lilies   of the spirit
that stirs the grasses   whirs hummingbirds'
wings   dances trees   leaps free

of the body's
                    complaint

Wishing in the Woods With Hillary

I wish you'd surprise me   in the woods   Hillary   as you did
that young mother   baby daughter on her back   the day after
                                             we lost you
for president   She took a selfie   My daughter sent me the link
Who will we be without you   in your moon bright pantsuit?
Who will stand up to the strongman   when Michelle and Barack
walk out of the White House   and speak to us only in dreams?

My wish is to see you among trees   their leaves gone gold
and crimson   or dry and dead on the earth   Your little dog
will sniff me   And you   who've been pilloried
your goodness debunked   as though working
for women and children   lacks gravitas   As though gravitas
is a loaded scrotum   whose natural enemy   is a woman with powers

Mother trudged from father's study   to kitchen   to bathroom
and back when he whistled   I kid you not   He whistled
                                             She typed
his manuscripts   cooked   bathed children   darned socks   Hillary
She was the air we breathed   the water we swam in
the earth we walked on   our hearth   our heartbeat
her powers invisible   to the kingdom of men   But O

she was fierce   about voting for you   in '08
Now she's lost   her way in the woods
lost my name   your fame   lost the whole world
of visible powers   lost to the outcry
the pandemonium   the kids walking out
of their schools shouting   "Not Our President"

The trees raise their boughs   and prophesy
When the moon comes closer to earth
than it's been since the year you were born

61

the haters will crawl out from under their rocks
the "white only" nation come out of the woodwork
You won't know whose country you're in

Maybe our time is over   Hillary   All that e-mail evil
because you're attached to your old familiar   that Blackberry
you refuse to waste time   learning new smartphones   I'm with you
But my dear   the world is passing us by   That young mother
in the woods   after we lost you for president   posted you
and her baby daughter on Facebook   It went viral
          My daughter sent me the link

Hillary   my wish is to surround you   with sisters
of the secret grove   We'll sit in a circle   kiss the earth
with our holiest lips   We'll lift up our hands and pray
for your healing   our healing   the healing of the dis–
respected   disaffected   molested   undocumented   Jim Crowed
And let's not forget   the trees   the bees   the buffalo

We'll breathe into our bellies   Our backbones grow
into strong tree trunks   our roots descend   While I'm wishing
let's throw in a chorus of frogs   and the smell
of the earth after rain   For it's downgoing time in America
underworld time   time to hide out in a cave
How I wish for your company in the dark   Hillary

We'll make a fire   talk story   remember our mothers'
invisible powers   Maybe we'll sink into dreamtime   Maybe
                                        Michelle
will visit   She'll wear a wonderful dress   remind us of grace   of joy
She'll speak from her heart   *Though the weather's becoming*
a banshee goddess   Though the "white only" nation
is trolling the web   Though the emperor elect

is tweeting our downfall   My wish is   Remember
The way of women   is our way   The moon swells
the moon goes dark   pulling the tides   in and out
The way of the trees   is our way   So raise up
your branches   sisters   for we are one   gathering
Soon sap   will rise   apple trees flower

We'll weave us a canopy   all over this land
It will be uprising time   once again
                                        in America

Her Song is in the Stars

Light plays on her face   as it does
on every baby's   Her fingers grip
                              an emptiness

                         There was surge
volcanic thrust   scream   and the sharp
edge of bone   The moon was full
of borrowed light   A big breath
blew it out   What had been

ocean   origin   beat of a strong
mother's heart   garment of flesh   was ripped
away   from this child   whose soft spot
was shaped by what ceased
                              to be

                   Where are the eyes
of her mother?   Her breasts   her warm belly
her laugh?   Who flung her song to the stars?

May her people wrap this child   in mother stories
tongue of the cat   shelter of wings
smell of the earth   after rain

and one day   when she's well along
in her years   has fought with her fate   given
and taken   gone down to the cellar
where roots are stored   may she come out into the light
in the early spring   in the blossoming trees
                         in distant delta   May she see
                                   her mother smile

Side Swiped

Sweet Lola   my Barcelona Red   hybrid   chariot
You   who transported me   from sixty something
to the middle of my seventies   through Obama's two terms
Michelle's organic gardens   the color spectrum
of her splendid gowns   you   carried me
when we were all   blind sided
by the 2016 election   fed me NPR news
the Russian hack job   on America
the wannabe Pharaoh   throwing tantrums
on Twitter   while traffic   roiled around us

even as you approached   a hundred thousand miles
you stayed stalwart   kept me safe   in your calm interior
as you switched   from gas to battery and back
making our small gesture   toward saving the planet
you who   delivered me   into our garage   protected
from rain   from wind   from the ash   that devoured the mountain
Dan coming out   to help   with the groceries

There were groceries   for Passover   in your trunk   Lola
flame raisins   dried apricots   dates   almonds
for the Sephardic Charoset   which symbolizes the mortar
it is said   we Jews used   to build the pyramids
when we were slaves   in Egypt   But who knew
when I made that left turn   a big black Beamer
would hurtle toward you   Lola   we almost
made it   before it hit you   in the right rear
I thought it was just   a fender bender
they'd fix you up   at the body shop
like the surgeon   fixed my hip

But the man in the Beamer   leapt out   shouting
It's all your   fault!
I can still hear him shouting

while his kind   quiet wife
asks for my registration

What's that?   I think
my mind   in fragments

Later I'll gather the flame raisins
dates   apricots and almonds   pulse them
into small bits   in the Cuisinart   knowing one needs
to break things up   to make that rich   sweet
middle eastern paste   that's meant to bind us   together
when vessels shatter

Later the total loss   claims man   will pronounce you
totaled   You   Lola
who had the *sechel* to feed your own battery   I'm still reaching
for your slow down lever   grasping thin air   forgetting
I'm driving a clunky   Chevy rental

on my way to retrieve   the layers of umbrellas   shopping bags
shoes in case of earthquakes   maps   we no longer use
flashlights   whose batteries likely died   in all those years
before you started   losing oil
before the black Beamer   side swiped you
before the man   began to shout

before the total loss man
pronounced you   worth more dead   dismembered
for spare parts   instead of resurrected   one last time
at the body shop   the buff young woman
commiserates with me   helps me carry
the detritus   of our years together
to the clunky Chevy

It's Easter week   and Passover
We remember the ones   whose passing
side swiped our lives   We light candles
for my children's father   Dan's children's mother
my mother   the bedlam that erupted   in her wake
O   my separated kin   will you ever   join us again?

We name the plagues Old Pharoah flings at us
as we gather our *mishpocha*   on the way to freedom
We name   what plagues our own   shattered   times

>   Stolen Elections
>   Separated Children
>   Hatred of Strangers
>   Greed
>   School Shootings   Sanctuary Shootings   Police Shootings
>   Street Shootings
>   Homelessness
>   Climate Chaos
>   Species Extinction
>
>   Family Feuds

The youngest one adds
>   *People who cannot forgive*

Pass the Charoset

To the Goddess of Ferment and Words

Yours is the river of tongues
we drink so we may remember

Yours the vines that grow words
the roots that dig down to old magic

Yours the arousal of green
the dazzle of yellow   the smell of purple

grapes in the sun
the song lines of blood

that dream in me still
of a tiger that prowls the realm

where words ferment
where a girl drinks the magic

Goddess she knows
but the Goddess she's not yet met

sits in a cave and has visions
of a girl who lives

in a white-haired woman
with that tiger   sometimes

she's ripped to shreds   sometimes
she's carried away

to the land where vines make music
where purple is crushed by our feet

where yellow descends to bless the wine
where the tiger snatches the girl by the nape

drags her to see her face in the pond
the face of the one she's become

a white-haired woman with notebook and pen
getting drunk on Your ferment
                                        of words

Self Portrait with Ghost

Are we to paint what's on the face, what's inside the face, or
what's behind it?

         – Pablo Picasso

If you should wander in from Beyond
with your hungry eyes and your brushes
How would you capture me now?

Your self-portrait from the bad years
holds my gaze   Look
My face has gathered angles   strong nose

for ghosts   like yours   dark brow
well versed in grief   a shock
of white mane I'd have you paint

like the crest of an Alp   were you here to see
how far I've come from that trembling
girl in a white dress with red flowers

from half a century ago   Yours was the time
of Picasso   It wasn't your work
to break the world open   to see

what's inside   It wasn't your way
to leap into myth with minotaur or clown   You painted
the outside   winter trees   family faces

I wonder   how would you capture what glows
in me now?   The burning snake
the dark lady   the lion who tracks

my sun and my rising   the egg I keep
in my pocket   like Jung
to smuggle the god across borders?

Maybe you'd paint me writing
Maybe you'd give me a backdrop
with crescent moons   cups and wands

mysterious Hebrew letters   Maybe
you'd sit me down by the window
let the tree shine in   as light from behind

a curtain   softens your face from
the bad years   Beyond all the grief
is the place   where your hungry eyes

still hold me   and poems begin

Your Nature and Mine

You   a poet of hiddenness   quote Bashō   *Learn about the pine*
from the pine   learn about the bamboo from the bamboo   You'd
have me write myself out of the poem   Or at most   be a
small figure   a bearded monk perhaps   at the foot of a great
mountain   *Let nature take over the poem*   is your teaching   *Be*
the rock the water falls over   the night blooming jasmine   the bees
the grasses   the rabbit in the grip of Great Horned claws at dusk

Look   the poem is *my* habitat   where *my* nature grows wild
I listen for what calls   I watch for what visits   Here comes
trouble   raccoon steals into the garden   makes a mess in the
compost bin   You'd be off walking the woods   notebook
stuffed in your pocket   Me?   I'm clanging the lids of my pots
to scare off the bandit   You   who step out of your self like an
old pair of jeans   return at dusk to see raccoon   tossing about
your pits and your peels   Raccoon lunges   You stand firm
taking notes   curious   Me?   I've retreated to my den   am
having it out with raccoon on paper   He gets the last word

It takes a good dose of chaos   to get creation going   That's where
                                                                    I come in

A Poet Changes Form

Direct me gods, whose changes are all holy
To where it flickers deep in grass, the moly
– Thom Gunn

Why haunt me now?   It's been a decade
since your final ride   on the horned god
Been half a century since our lives touched
briefly   You a master of British form
going to seed in America   Me   newly wed

lost to my own thread
If I could go back   find your craggy face
at some poetry reading   find my tongue   I'd say
Thom Gunn   You were my professor   back in the day
You couldn't have known how morning sick

I was   & how forlorn   But when you praised
my essay   on Mother Courage   sun sang
my name   earth gathered my feet
Let's be real   You'd have been
embarrassed   by such a blast of feeling   on a face

you don't quite   recognize   You'd have no patience
nor I the courage   for the real story   You
the prince of iambic pentameter   in biker boots
a far cry from my free verse lineage   or so
I thought   until I read your "Duncan"

I never knew how well you knew my Merlin
of the deep woods   never knew that you
and I   are creature kin   Holy Moly Thom
we dropped acid   in the same years
saw the flow of   "woods inside the wood"

on opposite sides   of the same bay
your "horns bud bright"   your feet turn hoof
as I go laughing down Euclid Avenue
pocketing bear paws   Ah Thom
you've changed form again   since I've meandered

your Shelf Life   you stride across America
in biker boots   ghost tripping
apple seeding in the wake of
Whitman   Williams   Duncan   Ginsberg
our "one all-river"   The truth is   I find it easier

talking to ghosts   & I am gathering my own
changed form   under your influence

God's Singing Tree

In Two Voices

When the forms are destroyed, the root is not destroyed.
— *The Kabbalah*

1. Ramban

I walk the Roman walls of your city   and the light
you received   from long before Moses
walks with me   through the narrow streets
of the Call de Jueu   This light is now

and you are in it   here on a tiny balcony
in the early evening   where church bells ring
each quarter hour   not far from the synagogue
no longer a synagogue   where they have made a library
in your name   (you who believed   in the oral transmission
you who argued   against writing it down)

Holy holy holy   is the word you were given
and your soul is bound up
in the light of the living ones

2. Ramban speaks

You don't know it 'til you lose it   the radiance
of a life   You are shaped by your times like bread
is braided for the Sabbath   and so it seems

it will always be like this   children playing peacefully
in the garden   the chant of the Shema   intertwined with
the bells of the cathedral   Who can say why

it changes   There is a shift   a rip   a disputation
is required   my knowledge is dangerous   and suddenly
I am an old man in exile   in Palestine
                              generations before
                                    the expulsion

We thought it was the end of time   but time went on
other countries   other ways   other tongues   Where
did the children of my children go   and the disciples
                                                of my disciples?

3. Dream Teaching

Ramban
does it trouble you
that I write down
what I hear you say?   Such pale reflections
of the mystery you teach   I need the written
word   for I have wandered and lost
my orientation   I have forgotten the names
of my ancestors   and that there is a secret
in our stories   Forgive me Ramban   if I stumble about
in the holy light   Forgive me if I stutter

   Ramban responds:
   You will stumble   for that is the way
   You will stutter   for how else does one say
   a mystery?   You will wrestle with my words
   in notebooks   on your strange new writing
   machine   Do not let yourself be stopped
   by some law you imagine   some tradition
   you don't think you understand   My daughter

   I have waited for you on the shining stair

   I was mute and ragged in your dream from years ago
   kept in the back shed   with the chickens and goats
   some yeshiva bocher   you did not know was in you
                                        kept me alive

   for you confused me with that rabbi in black robes
   who suffocated breath   drained light

76

stole magic   from the Torah
The congregation rose
sat down again   creaked chairs
shuffled feet   You believed
that sacred music belonged
to the Catholics   that ecstasy belonged
to the Sufis   that the breath of fire belonged
to the Hindus   that the tree goddess
who entered you   when you were a child
filled you   with her green joy
was an abomination in the eyes
of the fathers   No wonder you fled
No wonder it took you   most of a life
time   wandering   from Orissa to Thrace to Catalonia
to recognize me   that dancing rabbi in your dream
who threw you into the air
                              as a bride

4. God's Singing Tree

Ramban
you are old magic   with goddess eyes
you are warm fire   in the dark of the cave
you gather me back   to the breath of that mother
in the long long line   of my great grandmothers
who picked up her baby   her sack of food
and walked out of Catalonia   in 1492

The vessels shattered   There was contraction
there was exile   You tell me
this is the nature   of creation
          They who listen   will hear
          They who open their eyes   will see
          There is a tree   It grows from the feet
          of Abraham and Sara   Its leaves catch the light
          on this balcony   where I sit with you

77

Remember my daughter
wherever you are   the poem is
black fire written   on white fire
                    God's singing tree

Transport

The poem is my chariot   transported as I am
through mid-summer's long twilight   round the great round

         maiden
         maker
         ancestor

         back to the land of the swinging bridge
         ivy caves
         great mother oak
         where I was a wild horse girl

In those days   the voice of the father ruled
fear stirred the waters   lilies pulled petals in close

The poem was my chariot   the words knew the way
They were horses   out of a cave painting
            but when spooked
                my runaway chariot
                   plunged
                       into nightmare

         The castle crumbles
         Grandmother tiger slashes   my writing hand

         How's a girl to light the primal fire
         when Isis is
         a mound of pottery shards   and
         Sappho
         a forgotten mode of song   Yet

She sings to me   as ocean devours the sun
She sings to me   in measures of moon

for only the ancestors know
>how to slow those horses down
>slow breath
>slow heart
>gather my fragments to greet
>>first light

transported as I am
by every poem I've ever danced sung wrestled wrought
wrung out of harvest moons

Words are my horses   out of a cave painting
the chariot is made   of bone and tiger claw
Sappho takes the reins   She sings me through

midsummers' long twilight   round the great round

>maiden
>maker
>ancestor

>>across the swinging bridge

Section Three

Why Am I Here?

Why Am I Here?

Le Palais des Papes, Avignon, August 2018
for Marie–Laure

because this is the walled city   of the broken bridge
because I have been to the cave   seen the handprint of our
                         ancestor

                              waving   waving

                                        in red ochre
because mother is dead
             and I need a tincture   of my European essence
because I sit in a circle of strangers   we all speak alchemy
                   some of us speak Motherline

because the *mistral* blows fierce   all over Provence   will fling
          you down   knock you up

                              against the walls
because the Inquisition lasted five hundred years
because no one gets out of here alive
because we understand   this pompous pile of popery

                                   is Bluebeard's castle
because they herded up my ancestors   drove them into the fire
because the right wing is rising in the West   rules the East
because the plane trees have lost their bark

                              because of the drought
because there is no rescue   from overwhelm
          will Europa be savaged again
          like the blue spangled manikin   in the garden

                              without hands   without feet?

because we are all in the same boat
          all immigrants from Africa
          all fleeing some ancient terror
          all children of the children of the children
          of the grandmothers who knew   baking bread

is the sacred precinct   of the women   requires silence
no man dare intrude

because we are sitting on linens   our mothers' mothers embroidered
in the graveyards of Eastern Europe   listening
to their bones   their blood
because I belong to the grief   and the terrible stories
because I have been to the cave   and seen   the Paleolithic mare
from when poetry began
loping back into the dark

Ode to Frank O'Hara

I used to think you were not my type Frank   too fast a dancer
on too many glittering surfaces

         It was Ginsberg
who was my heart throb   when I was seventeen   O prophet
down from the mountain howling obscenities smashing taboos

But now that I am so much older
than you ever got to be   I crave the occasional ride
on the wings of your whimsy   to some place I remember
where poetry began   where sense is nonsense
after the long dream   of running through the jungle
stooping under vines   dodging venomous tongues
in the company of the bluesman
who is taking me home to meet his mother

I crave that intimate "you" of yours   as though you were saying
           tu or *du*
as though we were familiars lifetimes ago in a scene I dreamed up
to settle my stomach   in this time of narrowing straits   when
         truth   isn't truth
real   isn't real   you're a fresh draught of wonder   shifting
  my mood
  from Picasso's *tough quick axe*
  to the *glacier* in Bunny's *ear*
  you speak from your   *tight blue pants*
  and I can hear
      the sewage singing

On the way to the airport   the hills are as dry
as dandruff a single blow   from a hammer   could spark a
         firestorm
Are we talking vengeance? the Furies?   Are we talking the trees
reaching their claws down deep   into desperate rock?

desperate as the desperado   who snarls on social media
           doing his level best   to spark a race war

But Dan and I are going to Paris   Frank   as you did   in '58
as did we   in '88   in bodies as yet untouched by arthritis   with
                              souls not yet turned
inside out   by the rancor of robots   Long before
the mobster   took over the Oval   whose henchmen keep
                                           flipping
like upside down houses   like bandits with face paint   who rob us
                              at sword point
deep in the forest   on our way to Paris   night swallows morning
earth cantilevers the sky   we descend   into green and gold
                       swatches of fields bejeweled by trees

Awaiting our luggage
the ads look like windows   You're in them   looking *trés elegante*
                                           Frank
the Eiffel Tower   behind you   thanks to American Express
a child howls as time tangled gut mangled sleep severed as am I

Come on over here   Frank
      charm him   out of his tantrum   Make us all laugh!

Is the Universe Receiving?

We come with our begging bowls
we who were born for abundance
We ask only a star or two   a sliver of moon
We are hungry   Our souls are on empty

The mountain meanders the edge of the sky
coyote in late summer yellow   It's lonely   We're hungry
Distracted drivers are texting   traffic is snarling
When will we ever get home?

The Universe in her purple robes   is in no mood
to receive us   She's irritated   agitated   full
of catastrophes   Her rivers can't breathe   her whales
have gone sonar boom mad   her moons can't remember

their dreams   What does she want
us to do?   Empty our minds?   Chant?
Stand on the roof with the Dalai Lama?
Shut up and take our meds?

The mountain meanders the edge of the sky
coyote in late summer yellow   It's lonely   We're hungry
We who were born for abundance
come with our begging bowls   The Universe
                                    is in no mood to feed us

Your Dreaming Eyes

Have shown you such amazements   Remember?
The fox with turquoise teeth
The lion in the library of esoteric texts
The burning snake in summer grasses?   So why

has the maker of dreams
cast upon your eyelids *this* augury
of sea creatures?
The leaping spouting ones

ones who gather the sea to the land
who suckle their young   in shifting tides
who sing to their faraway kin
who companion your boat into dark waters

                             Gone   Gone   Gone

in a seizure of what?
Oil spill?   Algae bloom?   Detritus of plastic
Shopping bags?   Seas gone sour
with undigested dread?

Which Department of Ocean Management   will listen
to what your dreaming eyes report
What scientific study   with numbers   with graphs
can do right   by what's right in your face

A funeral barge piled high   Mass grave
for otters   seals   dolphins   whales
Desolation drifts by   closed eyelids
Who will companion your boat
                         into *these* dark waters?

Where the Buffalo Roam

A sky herd of buffalo   stampeded the moon   I saw it
driving on 24   The radio said

the shadow of earth   would steal the moon
our only moon   but I tell you

it was a thundering ghost herd   of buffalo
that shouldered the moon   out of her sky

The moon disappeared   in her deerskin dress
The ghost dancers stamped   and beat their drums

They chanted the world   before Highway 24
when earth was home   to the buffalo

when the people   followed the dance
of the sun   when they knew   each story of rock

each spirit of mountain   of tree
what flowered   what died   what came back

as the moon came back   in her deerskin dress
our only moon

In her radiant light
I looked at the sky over 24

But the buffalo were gone

Late Autumn Mountain

You are back
without fanfare
no trumpeting angel
no slow rising   red velvet curtain

just your blue bulk
on the day   after Thanksgiving
released   to my eyes
by the fall of leaves

You rise   in my sky
like a blue whale
like the word   of a god

and I bow to you   blessed as I am
by trees   filled as I am   with the loss
of gold   of auburn
                          drifting towards dust

Because the Mountain is My Companion

Because it meanders from coyote yellow
      to occasional green
Because we know that temperatures are rising
      we never expected this sudden freeze

Because the mountain   reached into cold wet skies   this morning
and gathered itself   a celestial garment   of snow
      as though it had ascended
      become an Alp
      a Himalaya

Because my tawny old Devil Mountain
      is a suddenly wild thing of snow and of ice
I try to put these things together   how green
      the hills glow along the freeway
on the news   the leaders of nations gather
      to argue about   carbon footprints
while in the city   dozens of red and white Santas
      mostly without umbrellas
      are gathering   in United Nations Plaza

Because the North Pole where Santa
      makes gifts
      is under water
and the Great White Bear   has walked to the end
      of his melting world

Because all our lives there's been some catastrophe
      just behind us
      just before us

You could hide under your desk   protect
      the back of your neck

or you could get in your car   and drive back
      to the mountain
      which has descended
      to its essential coyote yellow
      its occasional splashes of green

Because the mountain knows the eons in its bones
      it is a patient   broad shouldered bearer
      of wind   sun   rain   change

      I ask it to teach me   the long slow way

Patiann Rogers Comes to Mind During an Oil Spill

If I could bestow immortality
I'd do it liberally...on the night heron hatchling...
On the thrice–banded crab spider...
       – Patiann Rogers

If I knew as much science as you Patiann
knew migratory patterns mating rituals feeding behavior
of those creatures engulfed in sludge
they'd be in this poem   Would that help
those with feathers fouled by crude
those whose webbed feet can't swim
those with gaping mouths dead on the beach?

If I had your Audubon eye to describe how the least tern
sits on her eggs how the pelican makes her nest
Could we protect the hatchlings?   Could we rescue
the oil clogged sea turtle the soiled gull
the meandering crab dodging balls of tar with poems?

Me?   I get visions and their unbearable
music   There's a dragon fly with oil
weighted wings there's a blackened egret

This is a dirge for the blue fin tuna
They've lost their spawning grounds
in an ocean gone mad with black blood

If we could create an amulet Patiann
of feather and fin of marsh grass and the mystical measures
of dolphin song could we bring back the deep sea roe?

Or are we washed up too
                 in the Gulf?

Psalm for the Whales

the heaven is yours, the earth too
Psalm 89

Yours is the sun   awakening seeds
in the dark   They leap to the sky
as palm trees   bearing coconuts
as mangoes   thrusting flowers
into our hands

Yours are the roots   Yours the fervent
purple and pink bougainvillea   Yours the moon
whose fingers play with the tides

Yours the pelicans   dipping their wings
to touch you   Yours the mountains
who praise you   in rustling ferns
and in stone   Yours our eyes
which behold
you
feed us bananas   papayas   grapes
we learn to make wine

we who have walked on the moon
                    and sent pieces of metal to Mars
                              have forgotten

                    for everything taken
                              something   must be given back

The whales keep track
of our debt   They sing of blasts
under seas   of glaciers gone
to muck   of salmon that can't
                    make it home

          They sing and they sing   those whales
                              your prophets

On the Mexican Side of the American Wall

The mountains   old familiars   misty blue drifters   jungle
                                enfolded   they comfort us
and then   there's the sea   umbilical beat of the great mother's
                                                            heart

We've been coming here for twelve years   or is it thirteen?
                                          We've grown old
visiting this village   Only this time is different   America's
                                dream has been busted

The auction block   the shackles   show through   The Mexican
                                          president refuses
to meet with our incoming tyrant   Why should *he* pay   for
                                                    America's

twenty-billion-dollar wall?   We need sanctuary   At breakfast
                                      the Canadians wonder
"Why don't you just stay down here?"   We sat in this same

Great Hall   during the Bush years   watching the moods of the
                                                ocean and sky
the frigates soar   the pelicans swoop   and raged   about
                                government by the rich

for the rich   Shock and Awe   The treasures of Sumer looted
                              and lost   a culture destroyed
and all those young Americans   who came home   shattered
                                                shell shocked

This time is different   Bush would never have banned Muslims
                                  Anguish and rage
at the airports   on Facebook   on Twitter   in e-mails from every
                                              one we know

Someone says   "Government by fiat"   We wonder   Is it a coup?
Does he want power   for a billion years   like the former president
of Gambia?

Disconnect   Listen to the surf   Watch the palm trees wave their fronds
The talk is of sharks
The time he was swimming with his daughter   and someone
shouted "Great White!"

On the beach the waves are huge   surfers' delight   If we knew
how to ride waves   would that help?
The ocean opens her great goddess mouth   She raises her ancient
head   beats her fists on the sand

She's taking it back   our beach   for sandcastles   for baring our
breasts to the sun
for releasing baby turtles   protected by human children   as they
run   to the sea

Meanwhile in Berkeley   the students protest the Alt–right
When did that word arrive?   Anarchists dressed like Ninjas
invade Sproul Plaza   break glass   start fires   *Mario Savio*
Where are you now?

The bigot in chief would defund the University   First the
Muslims then the academics   *If mother*
hadn't lost her grip   on what's new   who's in charge   She'd feel like a
Jewish child   in Deutschland
all over again

We wander the beach   looking for ocean smoothed rocks   to fit
in the palm of a hand   to sooth a troubled soul   calm an angry
heart

At the lagoon   a congregation of turkey vultures   The ducks

flutter their wings   close
to hummingbird speed   They levitate   A dog leaps in and
out of the water   ecstatic

This is the lagoon   the local rich guy tried to hijack   fill it in
build a resort
The people said   "No!   You can't interfere with a waterway"
Standing Rock   in San Pancho

Bad night   Sleep slinks away   Mosquito bites itch   House
moans   *An Arab boy*
or is he Mexican   howls his fury   hurls his stones   at the big   bad
American wall

At the bar   David shows Julio how to make a Mezcal Martini
breaking down walls
with spirits   There is dancing in the streets of San Pancho   to
American Rock and Roll

The leader of the band   dedicates the next song to   "El Loco
en la Casa Blanca"
"Stop children   what's that sound?   Everybody look   what's
going down"

Come the Muslim registry   we'll be Muslims   What if we can't
travel?   What if we can never
come here again?   Where the sickle moon and Venus
commune in the velvet night

Where our days   fall into easy patterns   and we return   to our
old wild selves
Where every evening   we watch the sunset   You would not
believe the glory

we've seen   Imagine this   rays of sun through clouds   like a

                                       blessing   Sun disappears
in a streak of gray   is born again   dies again   is born yet again
                                       a glowing globe   and then
                                       the green flash

Medicine Wheel

1.

Each April   you lose sight of the mountain
as green leaves   take over the trees
You've been here before   and yet

Have you ever been round   such a wheel   of changes?
This time last year   you were gripped
by that agonized hip   Pain

was your shepherd   your cane   your walker
in the land   of the invalid   in the time
of medical marijuana   in the season of the Surgery

Waiting Room   You sat   among the resigned   the terrified
On the silent TV   the Man made of Greed   and his Hand-
                                                    maiden
descended the golden escalator

Hecate of the Crossroads   What do you see?

2.

This spring   it keeps raining   long past
the equinox   after how many seasons
of drought?   Your scar is healing

On a day blessed by sun   you and your Dan walk round
the reservoir   all the long   lovely   up and down of it
drinking in smells   and bird sightings

while the Wild Man of Mar-a-Lago
and the Fat Boy of Pyongyang
square off   with missiles

This is the spring Erdogan   steals Turkey
Maduro   sacks Venezuela   Le Pen looms
over Pax Europa   Putin's unmasked   as puppeteer

Kali   Lend us your Axe

3.

You are a woman   regaining your stride
You take to the streets   as though
the wheel turned back   to 1968

The Woman's March
The "Show Us Your Taxes March"
The March for Science   on Earth Day

The Stand Off at Standing Rock
The elders say   Water is Life
just ask the people of Flint

Just ask the people of Nogales   what a wall will do
to the Rio Grande   its flood plains   its families
its Mexican Gray Wolf

Blessed are they who wash the feet of the stranger

4.

This is the year you let go   the long horizon
At one   and at odds
in peace   and in pieces

astride Lady Fortuna's   wild wheel
in the grip   of the Man made of Greed
the danger that lives   in his eyes

Whomever he strikes   he strikes
in your name   Whoever strikes back
strikes you   and your sweet   beloveds

Destiny is a frayed rope
holding onto the boat
as seas rise

Mother of Changes   hold on to us

Most Stony South African God

In Suffering, and Nightmare,
I woke at last

to my own nature.
— Frank Bidart

Table Mountain
Knife Edge Mountain
Altar Mountain   where the Sacrifice is made
Most Stony South African God

you follow us   all over Cape Town
where Mandela   spoke to the crowd
We see You

at the Afro Cafe   in the alley
red roses   on orange and purple oil cloth
Black girl entwined   with her white lover
We see You

On Robben Island,
where the writing on the wall reads
"Happy Days are Here Again!"
Derrick says he's still imprisoned
can't get a job   besides this
being our tour guide   in Maximum Security
We see You

At Langa   where Brenda and her sons
share six dark rooms   one stove   one broken toilet
with fifteen other families
You have our number

At the Langa Baptist church
held in the murmur of prayer

in Xhosa   in English
we call you JESUS   HALLELUJAH
Forgive us for what we have done
Forgive us for what we have not

Table Mountain
Knife Edge Mountain
Altar where the Sacrifice is made   You Saw

WHAT THEY DID
TO STEVEN BIKO.
How the GIRL   GOT BURNT.
How the HEART   SLUNK AWAY
What did we know?
What did we not know?

O mountain
pull your cloud about you
gnash your teeth!
You've got our number

Kitchen   Table Mountain
sit us down with those
we'll never understand
Make betrayer   meet betrayer
Make us eat   our own maggoty stories

WHEN THE MOTHERS
LOOKED INTO THE FACES OF THEIR SONS'
MURDERERS   FOUND THE HUMAN
                                                    CORD
                                            Where does it live?
                                            Such Forgiveness?

What do we know?
What do we not know?

Wise mountain
Dumb mountain
TOOTHLESS MOUNTAIN
GRINNING SKULL MOUNTAIN

Most Stony South African God
You've got our number
Follow us home

Sam and Sara In the Land of Ash

Ending with a line from Gwendolyn Brooks.

Don't go out when the sun burns red
when the air hangs thick   with smoke   chokes
the mountain   gropes the valley   shreds your lungs
    with shattered shelter

Don't go out in the nightmare night
in the whirlwind breath   of some devil's spawn
Power lines spit   Fire ball   leaps
                    Where

is sanctuary   when home is gone?
your flowers in vases   your tall standing Buddha
your journals   your paintings   your baby
                       pictures

the Monterey pines   that sang
your comings   your goings
your shoes in a rack
            by the door

Don't try to hide   in that old hippy house
tie die skirts   purple shawls
detritus   from the yellow submarine
            A house

you know only   in dreams   It moans   It groans
We never imagined this world   The furies
of weather   of speed   of greed
        and Dr King's dream

as gone   as Walter Scott   shot
eight times in the back
while running away
        unarmed

In the land
of the Great God Gun   In the land
of the Great God Hate and you wake
to knocking   at your door   to pounding
            in your heart

to the sight of an ominous glow on the ridge   and the night
of exploding trees   melting plastic
poison gases   smashed

                              rememberings

911 says
There's fire   after fire   after fire
There's no way we can get to you
                        We're so sorry

Is it the fire   this time?   Are we goners?   Where
is sanctuary?   It is time
to call   your family   say
            goodbye

        Drive
says the one who knows   the story of fire   *Keep driving*
from black spot   to black spot
where the earth has already
        been burned

You reach for the ghost   of the kettle   the manuscript
the paintbrush   the jacket   the pillow   all gone
into the luminous black
        of Ohm

This is the story of two
come through   the land of ash
Now build your altar   on black   burned   ground
                "with love like lion—eyes"

Pearly Girl the Spirit Dog

What brings you to my dream   old dog
of my children's   childhood?   We slog
through desolation   among the bruised
the bereft   Escaping what?   It's twilight

and you   tugging at the leash   comfort me
What happened here?   Where are the grasses
the trees?   Was it wildfire   drought
nuclear waste burning underground?

Was it mass shootings   hate mongering
the buffalo demon   Durga's revenge?   She
whose form is shadow   She
who is Mother Earth   turned nightmare

Sweet Pearl   our pit bull protector
before we lost the war
on poverty   before bloodied
classrooms   burning towers   the massacre

of civil rights   the resurrection
of Jim Crow   before
artificial intelligence   assaulted
                              the world soul

You follow some track   I can't
comprehend   your dogged nose
to the ground   and I remember
back in our prime   the kids kept fighting

You got between them   and barked   till they stopped
I got entangled   in Yama's dread hair   until She
who releases women   rode in   on her lion

You   pricked up your ears   to hear my songs

of the wild world   where dreams are
$$\text{the north star}$$

where a horse leaps out   of a cave painting
where the Mother of the Mountain   kisses me
full   on the lips   and you
dog of my dreams

vault over my house   like the cow
$$\text{that jumped over the moon}$$

Stay by me   Pearly Girl   Great Spirit
I need the nose   of your knowing
to follow the scent   of the buffalo demon
from outrage   to sorrow

dream to dream   poem to poem
smell fear   smell rot
smell hot blood   smell rain
all the way to the bottom   of down

the river's edge   where Yama waits
$$\text{His red eyes glow}$$
$$\text{in the dark}$$

Ghost Without Story

      for Nikki

Even now in the dusk when I call you who wandered away so young
leaving your teeth
                your bones
                      your long flowing hair
                      your black and white photos
    of when we were
          lovely   lost
                full of doorways
                        arches
                              stairways to where?

Even now that the children have children that the young have
                                    grown old
that my dead surround me grandmothers   lovers   girl friends
                                    who visit
              when sun strikes the willows

All except you who refuse me again
I startled you once a black cat stalking a dove   I dreamt you
were a large green snake   I've made offerings

bowls of red cherries and plums for the summers you lost
baskets of pears and persimmons for fall
I've gathered you tiger lilies

You're not interested   Some of you dead just refuse to be fed
And anyway what can be said to the Queen
of high heeled boots and flung crockery

about this slow walk round the labyrinth the ins and outs
of stones and abalone shells   How the center found me
      How the tug

of the earth   has gathered my feet

Even now you refuse to hear
the question I've carried for years   It flutters in my hands   flies off
with your irritated mutter

> *Let dead ends be dead*
> *Let a ghost be a ghost without story*

When One of Us Is Ripped Loose We All Unravel

For Jessica

I remember your glow   Jessica
back in the day   when we gathered
in your barn   for the drumming

Drum found me   Found breath
Found pulse   Found vision   the White Wolf
She visits me still

Where was She   the White Wolf
when the holy cup of you   spilled
on a bend of Highway 1?   What happened

between your car   that road   that tree?

How many shapes   can a spirit take
when suddenly ripped   from the flesh?
Seed mother   lettuce grower   vision seeker

bright root

In my dream   you are a black sheep
grazing on sky blue   forget–me–nots
We are such mysteries to one another

The holy cup of you   has spilt among us

Lady of greens   your spirit
rattles our fences
beats a drum   with our bones

Who drank too much   of whose cup?

Who crossed over   whose line?
Who squandered the harvest?   What happened

between your car   that road   that tree?

If I should arrive
at that bend in the road,
will the White Wolf appear?

The holy cup of you   has spilt among us

Since Don Sandner Left His Body

He knew what to do   with an eagle feather
how to sweep clean   the air around us
clear our heads   of angry noise
as we entered the barn

We lay   on sweet smelling grasses
we who'd been smudged   who'd been purified
and he beat and he beat and he beat on that drum
we thought it was forever   the White Wolf appeared

Those who know   the animals
who know feather sweep   drum beat
corn dance   how the people shift
from one foot   to the other

know there is a place   for each one
coyote   snake   rock   child
So the White Wolf   sings to the hills
so she sings to the fire   we sit around

we who are left

The truth is
we've never been the same
since he left his body   so suddenly
teeth   of the alligator

scissors   of mind
rocks   severed   from gods
trees cut down
        cut down   are we lost?

Nobody   beats the drum
Nobody   sweeps clear the air
Nobody   remembers the dance
Nobody   is a dark cave

where the White Wolf

still lives
                    See?
She lifts her head to the mountain
                                        She pricks up her ears

The Green One

has taken up residence
in my garden   bursts out
of the pruned roses   tosses laughter
into the fountain   flings hummingbirds

into the shimmering   He disdains
the clock   insists it's time
for me to learn   his dervish whirl
in the meadow after rain   He has no patience

for my aching joints   forgetting I'm no
excited toddler   reaching for the bright
beyond the trees   He refuses to distinguish
between this life

and the ones I have imagined
the ones I've dreamt
in which I wander   ancient lands
hand in hand with   The Green One

who lets the sun   into my winter cave
who whirls me out   of time's confines
who makes the sap rise
who makes the lilies of the valley   speak

in their forgotten tongues   He's crow
on a branch above my head   He laughs
because I don't know how
to ride   the rapture currents

to the thunder world   He leaves me dazed
confused and soaking wet   then rides by   on a camel
scoops me up   carries me to his tent   his hookah visions
of a garden   with a fountain laughing

among roses   a hummingbird that hovers
in the shimmering   and I am
an excited toddler
reaching for the bright beyond

                              the trees

Glacial Blue

I.

Getting lost is my strong suit   I can get lost
between the bathroom   and the piano lounge
in the cruise ship   where my man waits
He always knows   where he is   But the years
have shown me   getting lost is the only way
to see Venice   to catch the music   of the poem beginning
to limp into that back country   where getting old
and getting lost   are one and the same   It's the way
of the labyrinth   as though wandering the gut
of the Venetian Lion   confounded and confused   until
coming round the bend   there it is

sunlight   and the Grand Canal

II.

In our stateroom   mirrors reflect mirrors
I can see the back of my head   My hair grows
in circles   So do our voyages   around the sun
around the earth   around the Black Hole
Our ship sits in the mouth   of Disenchantment Bay
named by a lost sea captain   looking for
the North West Passage   We've come to see
the glacier   famous for surging   It dammed up a fjord
created a lake   trapped animals   calved blue icebergs
threatened ships   This morning
it refuses to be seen   is cloaked in fog   The ancestors
drift in   telling stories   of the Inside Passage
Maybe it's time   to let it all go
your Russian name   your German boots   your Jewish angst

III.

From the still eye   in the center of the spiral   I see
my Russian grandmother   known to me only

in the photo　　Her drooping eyelid　her inward gaze
It's late fall　1942　　She's dying　in a transit camp
Her soul　a drift of glacial blue　reaches out　to me
delivered　into the light　by Dr Stern　　He pulls too hard
on my left shoulder　　Dislocated
by birth　into a dislocated family

IV.

I married a voyager　our years bejeweled
by the journeys he crafts　　Mostly we travel South
Mexico　Southern Europe　Southern Africa　Southern India
But as we lose　the world we know　　As the news cycle
spins continuous sagas　of skullduggery　thuggery
every day a new catastrophe　while Google
plots Augmented Reality　and the Internet of Things
hands us over　to the 'bots　　I hear a voice say　　*Maybe it's time*
to get lost　due North　where you've never been before　time
for the Inside Passage　to mist your soul with glacial blue　time
for the pull of the mountains　lifting your gaze　to grave
and granite elders　streaked with snow　　Maybe it's time
for the humpbacked whale　　She blows　breaches　displays
her flukes　here in the feeding grounds of her youth　　Time
for a pair of bald eagles　mated for life
guarding their young in a Sitka Spruce
When courting　it's said　they link talons　spiral down
in a mid air dance　　Let each other go　just in time
to keep from crashing　　Maybe it's time
to visit the gods　who live here　among the people
of the tides　and the earthquakes　among the ravens
and the eagles　the bears and the whales　　They speak little
wear a bemused expression　on their animal faces
their rock faces　　They will not answer your questions
about fast glacial flow　or the Black Hole　　Maybe it's time
to trade it all in　your Russian name　your German boots
your Jewish angst　for wilderness　　If you're lucky

the mountain   the high one   the sacred one   will rise above everything
This is not story   not history   This is pure being
in icy stone stillness   in constant flux
in silence   in endless summer solstice light
rainforest   tundra   wolf   caribou
Northern Hawk Owl   all that
the glaciers have wrought
                              in their passing

The Queen of Souls

Some souls are shy   They hide out   behind the shutters   of
                                                    your eyes
Some souls are soggy   like the earth after rain   like a woman
                                            after a good cry
Some souls get born to sass the universe   listen to them snicker
                                    in the back of the class

Some souls can never be satisfied   Give them three wishes
                                                    they want five
They eat your heart out   send your spirit packing   You forget
            who brought you here   You question your every breath
                        your spirit guides   your mother's milk

Some souls have rocks in their shoes   drag you down
to the bottom of the slough   where earth worms squirm
and you are sunk   spat out   for what terrible deed
                                            in what former life?

Some souls insist   on dance   Some need poems   Some will
                                                    make you
map out a whole world   of characters   who'll take over
your inner chambers   Won't stop talking   until you write
                                                    them down

Some souls keep singing   even in the eye of the storm   even at
                                                    the bottom
of the pit   where the Queen of Souls   She who harrows your
                                            bones   knows
even black holes   even dead trees   grow mushrooms   host
                                    baby birds   and snakes

Some souls live in sand castles
until a wave   knocks them down
The child forgets   what she built

Some souls have feathers   and claws
Some souls can shed   their skin
Some souls become jaguars   in your sleep

Some souls surf atmospheric rivers   wrangle tornadoes
ride nightmares   glide and glitter
amidst rays of the sun   in the redwood grove

Some souls are old   and lonely   Can't remember
                                        the last body
                                              they were in

They hover in the rafters   watch the infinity loop
of lovers   impatient for that final   passion cry
for the deft dive   of sperm into egg   hungry to leap
                                              into new life

Some souls remember themselves   as tears   as pearls
on the throat   of the Queen of Souls
When your time comes   She'll weigh

your heart   your balance   of feather   and claw
Maybe She'll give you   a glimpse
of your soul's flight   wings aflame
                              on the way   to your stars

About the Author

Naomi Ruth Lowinsky's soul was shaped by deep impressions made on her by India, where she lived for two years in the 1960s. It was there the Goddess claimed her. It was there that myths began singing to her. It was there her soul remembered other lives. It was there her stars insisted she learn to tend her fire. And the fire spoke: *I am the heat of your passion. It is I who will show you your way.* What to do on her return to America but become a Jungian, and a poet?

Lowinsky won the *synkroniciti magazine* "Space" prize, and was nominated for a Pushcart Prize. She also won the Blue Light Poetry Prize, the Obama Millennial Award and is an International Merit Award Winner in the Atlanta Review 2020 Poetry contest. *Your Face in the Fire* is her sixth poetry collection.

Lowinsky is a Jungian Analyst, a member of the San Francisco Jung Institute, and poetry editor for *Psychological Perspectives.* She has led a poetry workshop, *Deep River,* for many years at the San Francisco Jung Institute and co-edited an anthology of poems by its participants, *Soul Making in the Valley of the Shadow.* She blogs about poetry and life at sisterfrombelow.com.

Acknowledgements

I owe my deepest gratitude to many who are gone from this world, who were mentors, teachers, friends and believers in my work. Among them are Diane di Prima, Thom Gunn, Betty Meador, Elizabeth Osterman, Don Sandner, Gilda Frantz, Robin Robertson, Margaret Ryan, John Gardner, my mother, Gretel Lowinsky, and my brother, Si Lowinsky.

Among the living I am forever grateful to Susan Terris for her exquisite eye and ear for the organization of this book, to my publisher, Diane Frank for her enthusiasm and generosity, and to Melanie Gendron for her visionary book design. I am grateful to Judy Grahn for her inspiration so long ago. Many thanks to Richard Messer, often my first reader, and the poets of Deep River, also early readers, who have helped me craft many poems.

Deep gratitude to Kathleen Russ, who, by an amazing synchronicity, sent me her remarkable painting, and gave me permission to use it for the cover of this book.

Most of all thanks to my husband, Dan Safran, who listens to early drafts with an open heart and a good ear, sends out submissions, and has been a loving companion and a grounded reality check on our many – inner and outer – journeys.

Many thanks to the editors of the following publications, in which some of these poems have appeared, often in earlier versions.

After the Pause: "On the Mexican Side of the American Wall," "Wishing in the Woods with Hillary"

The Book of Now: "Because the Mountain is My Companion," "Patiann Rogers Comes to Mind," "Where the Buffalo Roam"

DecomPmagazine: "Self-Portrait with Ghost"

Drunk Monkeys: "To the Lady and Her Poet"

Eclipse: "Because of What Aches"

Evening Street Review: "To a Kinsman"

Front Porch: Birth Day

The Gathering: 11: ""To My Long Ago Lady Delight"

Ginosko: "Fire Is Your Name and Your Maker," "In the School of Desire"

Jewish Women's Literary Annual: "Memory   Old Trickster"

Juked: "Serenissima's Embrace"

Jung Journal: "Since Don Sandner Left His Body"

Left Curve: "Most Stony South African God"

Minetta Review: "The Green One"

New Millennium Writings: "Will the Universe Receive Us?" "Why Am I Here?" (Honorable Mention)

Oberon: "Pearly Girl the Spirit Dog"

Origins: "Glacial Blue," "Medicine Wheel"

Psychological Perspectives: To the Goddess of Ferment and Words," "Me Too," "God's Singing Tree"

Qwerty: "To My Brother's Late Dragon Lady, "Your Nature and Mine""

Schuykill Journal of the Arts: "Late Autumn Mountain"

Sierra Nevada Review: "Late in Love"

Soundings East: "What She Says to Her Old Mother India"

Spillway: "Only the Blind"

Straight Forward: "Banshee Under Your Skin"

Terror, Violence and the Impulse to Destroy: "Your Face in the Fire," originally published as "Psalm" in the essay "Wrestling with God.

Tiferet: "Thanks"

Tiger's Eye: "Your Dreaming Eyes"

Westview: "Psalm for the Whales"

Whistling Shade: "Angelology"

Wild Violet: "Lust and the Holy"

Wrath-Bearing Tree: "Side Swiped," "Queen of Souls"

Notes

"The State of California" section 6. Influenced by Judy Grahn's book, *Blood Bread and Roses: How Menstruation Created the World.*

"Full Circle with Goddess." Quotes in bold are from Judy Grahn's Graphic Book of Poems, *She Who.* Oakland: Diana Press, 1972.

"Me Too" addresses Christine Blasey Ford as she testified against the nomination of Brett Kavanaugh to the Supreme Court.

"Banshee Under Your Skin" refers to an ancient women's ritual, the Thesmophoria, which is described in Betty De Shong Meador's book, *Uncursing the Dark.*

"God's Singing Tree." Ramban is the familiar name given the medieval Kabbalist, Moses ben Nachman of Catalonia.

Printed in the USA
CPSIA information can be obtained
at www.ICGtesting.com
LVHW090350150624
783218LV00017B/44